About Glasgow

By John Struthers

The quotes in this book on Glasgow's renaissance from famous people in all walks of life are testament in themselves to the success of the Glasgow's Miles Better campaign.

All of the quotes have been freely given with best wishes from the people concerned.

The quotes attributed to Her Majesty The Queen and The Prince of Wales have been taken from speeches given by Her Majesty and Prince Charles who kindly gave permission for their use.

Particular thanks is expressed to all the people who have contributed their time, materials and efforts to this book. They represent the spirit that has made Glasgow's renaissance possible.

Acknowledgements

Bookbinder:
James Gowans Ltd

Colour separations:
Arneg Ltd
CMR Graphics Ltd
Reproscan (Scotland) Ltd

Paper:
Donald Murray (Paper) Ltd

Photography:
The Albany Hotel
The Briggait
British Caledonian Airways
Joe Campbell
Randolph Caughie
Bill Cooper
The Daily Record
Richard Ellis
Stephen Gibson
Glasgow Chamber of Commerce
Glasgow District Council
Glasgow Garden Festival
The Glasgow Herald
Glasgow Museums & Art Galleries
Glasgow School of Art
Trevor Graham
Mike Henderson
Holiday Inn, Glasgow
Hospitality Inn
Kings Theatre
Finlay Martin
Paul Mellon
The Mitchell Library
Brian Morgan
Wm Nimmo & Partners
The North Face
John Pierce/Photosport International
David Riach
ScotRail
Scottish Ballet
Scottish Development Agency
Scottish Exhibition & Conference Centre
Scottish National Orchestra
Scottish Opera
Scottish Television
Scottish Tourist Board
Sportapic
Stakis Grosvenor Hotel
Tony Stone Associates
John Struthers
Eric Thorburn
University of Glasgow

Typesetting:
The Davidson van Breugel Creative Group

They said it

Her Majesty The Queen

H R H The Prince of Wales

Archbishop of Canterbury
Jeffrey Archer
Stanley Baxter
Sir Terence Beckett
Ian Botham
Janet Brown
Bobby Charlton
Robbie Coltrane
Tom Conti
Ronnie Corbett
Kenny Dalglish
Lord Forte
Sir Campbell Fraser
Russell Grant
Rt Hon Robert Gray
Jimmy Greaves
Rt Hon Lord Hailsham
Sir Peter Hall
Rt Hon Sir Michael Havers
Rt Hon Michael Heseltine
Tony Jacklin
Gordon Jackson
Rt Hon Roy Jenkins
Sir John Harvey-Jones
Rt Hon Neil Kinnock
The Krankies
Lulu
Sandy Lyle
Andrew Neil
Rt Hon David Owen
The Pope
Rt Hon Malcolm Rifkind
Diana Rigg
B A Robertson
Jean Rook
Willie Rushton
Selina Scott
Very Rev Dr Smith
Rt Hon David Steel
Rt Hon Donald Stewart
Rt Hon Margaret Thatcher
Sir Adam Thomson
Frankie Vaughan
Ian Wallace
Molly Weir
Allan Wells
Rt Hon Shirley Williams
Rt Hon George Younger

Printed by J Thomson Colour Printers Ltd
14 Carnoustie Place, Glasgow G5 8PB

© Published by Struthers Advertising & Marketing Ltd
Struthers House, 8 Claremont Terrace
Glasgow G3 7XR

First published 1986

Designed by John Struthers

ISBN 0 9511851 0 1

They said it

To John Andrew

With Best Wishes

John Struthers

March 1988.

Contents

10 DOWNING STREET

THE PRIME MINISTER

The people of Glasgow, whose forefathers pioneered trade routes around the world and engaged in extraordinary feats of engineering in distant countries are now putting these same qualities to work in successfully transforming Glasgow itself into a city equipped to meet the challenges of today.

Much has been done, and though there is still much to do, the evidence of change, of progress, of sheer dogged determination and hard work is there for all to see. Look around at the old, restored and renovated, marching in step with the new and the innovative. Enjoy the art galleries and museums with their world famous collections. Sample the opera, the music, the theatre, the ballet. Walk in the beautiful parks and gardens which lie both in and around the city.

But most importantly, talk to the people. You will find them fiercely proud of their city, and rightly so.

They will tell you in no uncertain terms, why they say Glasgow's miles better.

Margaret Thatcher

Telling the world about Glasgow

The campaign to tell the world that Glasgow's Miles Better was launched in 1983 by Dr Michael Kelly, the then Lord Provost of Glasgow. It was a campaign devised to correct the many misconceptions of how Glasgow was perceived outside of the city. We believed that the city's image was out-dated, inaccurate and unfair and that a determined and prolonged effort should be made to improve it, with the very many obvious benefits that would be derived from a successful campaign.

We knew from a study of other cities throughout the world and particularly New York that their "I love New York" campaign had radically improved that city's image and contributed enormously to investment and tourism with their huge spin-off benefits.

In fact, the seed was sown for a Glasgow campaign in September 1982, when as head of one of Scotland's most successful advertising agencies, I had made an approach to the Lord Provost, whom I had not met until that time, with the specific purpose of selling him the idea of our services in the promotional field on behalf of Glasgow. Indeed, our very first job for the city, the design of the Lord Provost's Christmas card, was the forerunner in starting to change one very important misconception of how the world at large thought we conducted ourselves in Glasgow! That Christmas card, which received much acclaim from all corners of the globe, showed on its front cover The Pope shaking hands with the Moderator of the General Assembly of The Church of Scotland, with a verse from Longfellow's poem "Peace on Earth" reproduced inside the card. It was a sentiment to which we all subscribe.

Our second job for the City, devising the Glasgow's Miles Better campaign and creating the marketing strategy that would sell it to the world, proved to have a major stumbling block. There were, in fact, no funds available from any source to finance the campaign. If there was to be a campaign, it would clearly require to be financed in its initial stages by Struthers Advertising; a most unusual situation for an advertising agency to find itself with an idea but effectively no client, nor funds to implement it! However, we have never been short on initiative in Glasgow and I took the decision to underwrite the campaign; the rest is history.

The first principle would be to develop the campaign concept and bring it to a stage where it would be professionally presented to likely

The Lord Provost's Christmas card received much acclaim from around the world. It shows the Pope shaking hands with the Moderator of the General Assembly of the Church of Scotland and proclaiming the message "Peace on Earth"

sources of finance for a long term promotion. With that in mind, we made a promotional video which encapsulated the strategy for the campaign, introduced the slogan Glasgow's Miles Better but most of all outlined the absolute necessity for Glasgow to get out and sell itself to the world. That video was the first shot fired at a target audience which consisted of Glasgow Businessmen and anyone with a vital interest in the future of Glasgow.

The video was shown for the first time in the City Chambers to the invited audience early in 1983 and indeed was overwhelmingly welcomed by the entire assembly. The media support was equally overwhelming and enthusiastically welcomed. The Evening Times said "The Glasgow's Miles Better campaign is one of the best ideas ever to have come out of the city"; The Scottish Daily Express said "All of Scotland has much to gain from the Glasgow's Miles Better campaign. Getting the right image is a giant step to reaping rewards and the whole of Scotland will welcome this unique enterprise." Funds started rolling in and the campaign was under way. The subsequent co-operation between the private and public sectors of the community has been described as a partnership of success, unique to Glasgow. The District Council has also contributed some £50,000 each year to the campaign funds and there is now a formal Miles Better Committee which is chaired by Lord Provost Robert Gray. The initial rallying video went on to win a major international award at the New York International Film and Television Festival in 1983, as did the two subsequent promotional videos in 1984 and 1985.

Our very first objective at the launch of the campaign was to get the people of Glasgow behind us. In fact, the slogan itself "Glasgow's Miles Better" almost immediately achieved this. The slogan undoubtedly reflected that Glasgow people are happy, friendly and smile a lot. Smiles Better or Miles Better? Miles Better than what? The answer was probably best summarised by BBC's Frank Bough when he said "It's an ingenious slogan, you can either read it as Smiles Better or Miles Better, very clever."

Obviously the slogan had to make a statement which projected our message in a memorable and catchy way and few could dispute that the slogan is very positive in that context. In fact, it was in effect saying

Glasgow is "much improved" or "miles better than it was". It quite clearly projected our message with fun and succinctly in three words, the very essence of a good slogan. Indeed when I presented the campaign to the Lord Provost in the City Chambers in 1983 his precise words on it were "I love it". And when the campaign was launched in London, the Lord Mayor of London, Lady Donaldson said "This campaign is a brilliant idea". Funnily enough, the campaign was conceived on Lady Donaldson's own doorstep and the slogan was actually written as my eleven year old son Mark and I, travelling on the London tube, after spending the journey from Glasgow discussing the campaign.

My first thought on arriving at the "words" was to put a visual smile in Glasgow to reflect our friendly message and my second thought was, why not put Mr Happy himself in Glasgow? It seemed the perfect answer, and as coincidence would have it, the creator of the Mister Men cartoon characters, Roger Hargreaves, had actually worked in the same London advertising agency as myself some years previously. One phone call to Roger and Mr Happy was recruited for service in Glasgow! He has since been adopted by the people of Glasgow who have now proudly displayed more than a million car stickers with Glasgow's message travelling the world. Glasgow's pride has certainly been restored.

The mainstream of the campaign has been carefully targetted at decision makers and people who influence them. If we are to change perceptions and achieve our objectives we must sell ourselves to people who can bring about change; the people who will direct investment to our city and expand the economy. Sophisticated colour magazine advertisements have played a large part in this direction and will continue to do so. Our job is to tell and convince these people that Glasgow IS indeed miles better. And that is not difficult because Glasgow is a superb product with a lot to offer.

There is, I believe, considerable evidence of our success on which we must continue to build. That success is perhaps best summarised by The Sunday Times who said "Glasgow has of course achieved a tremendous turnaround in the last five years. The catchy "Glasgow's Miles Better" ad campaign has helped remove the grimy, crime-ridden image: more people are realising that Glasgow is perhaps the most interesting city in the British Isles." Clearly, perceptions are changing.

Spreading Glasgow's message around the world. The picture opposite shows Struan and Graeme Rafferty on holiday in Spain, proudly displaying Mr Happy and Glasgow's Miles Better.

The Burrell Collection

On November 27, 1985 Her Majesty The Queen said in her opening speech at the Scottish Exhibition Centre "In recent years, I am happy to say, visits to Glasgow for major events have become something of a habit with me. The Glasgow Underground, the Regional Council Headquarters, The Chamber of Commerce, the Glasgow Herald and most recently, the Burrell Collection — these are just some of the items which have appeared in my Scottish programme since 1979. They go to show that your city, at a time of general economic difficulty, continues its great tradition of looking to the future, at the same time paying proper respect to its past."

It was in October 1983 that she had again paid tribute to Glasgow at the opening of the Burrell Collection when she said "Glaswegians can be proud, not only of Sir William Burrell and his astute and unflagging pursuit of excellence, but also of the way in which they have responded to his generosity. He himself could not have visualized a finer setting for the Museum than Pollok Park, the gift of the Maxwell MacDonald family, without which the search for a home might still be going on. Difficulties which could have daunted people of lesser mettle have been overcome and the collection is now permanently housed in a building worthy of it. I congratulate all those who have, over the years, worked to achieve this in so many ways — Trustees, Councillors, Architects, Contractors, Museum Administrators and Staff.

Today's occasion offers further proof, if it is needed, that Glasgow

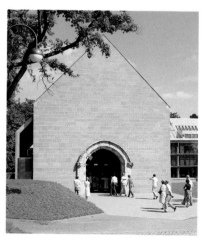

leads from the front in matters artistic. I am sure that people will flock to Pollok Park from all over the world and see for themselves the warm smile on Glasgow's face.''

In fact, the Queen's prediction could not have been more accurate. Since the Burrell opened in 1983, it has been overwhelmingly popular and people have flocked to Pollok Park from every corner of the globe. It has been a resounding success and has most certainly contributed to the "smile on Glasgow's face."

Indeed, its popularity can be measured by the fact that it has become Scotland's number one tourist attraction, even surpassing visitors to Edinburgh Castle. Perhaps not surprising when one considers the magnificence of the Collection which prompted R W Apple Jnr to write in The New York Times "The Burrell Collection is one of the most remarkable assemblages of works of art ever brought together.''

The Burrell is certainly a collection that is truly unique and breathtaking. Bequeathed to the city in 1944 by Sir William Burrell, the collection embraces paintings, sculpture, tapestries, silver, ceramics, stained glass and furniture, representing some 8,000 items over 4,000 years of artistic activity — medieval tapestries to pastels by Degas, finest Chinese ceramics to classical antiques. And housed in one of the most glorious new buildings in Britain, specially designed for the Collection by Barry Gasson it proves beyond all doubt that Architecture is in itself an art form. It's a perfect building for the collection.

There is no doubt that the glass-walled building is in itself a masterpiece, almost perfectly blending with the quite beautiful Pollok Park near the city centre and totally accomplishing the brief to display the Collection for all to enjoy and experience and where care has been taken to preserve the remaining records of civilisation for future generations.

Sir William would certainly be very proud if he could see the resting place for his outstanding Collection, with the knowledge that it was being enjoyed by the world at large and carefully, lovingly looked after by the people of Glasgow for whom he had so much affection. He would have derived enormous pleasure, as did all of Glasgow, when on the opening day of the Burrell the Glasgow Evening Times said in its leading article "Glasgow was today confirmed as one of the leading art centres of the world," lending weight to the kind words of Her Majesty The Queen.

Above: Sir William Burrell.
Top left: Polychrome horse and figure,
Tang Dynasty.
Top centre: Tapestry, detail from
Luttrell Table Carpet.
Top right: Degas, Jockeys in the rain.
Centre left: Rembrandt van Rijn, Abraham
Francen, Apothecary.
Centre: Lucas Cranach the Elder,
The Stag Hunt.
Centre right: Antoine le Nain, peasant children.
Bottom left: Rodin, The Thinker.
Bottom right: Eugène Boudin, The Empress
Eugénie on the beach at Trouville.

A new Glasgow — and miles better

" I stumbled off a sleeper one cold morning in November and thought I must have the wrong stop. But no, from Central Station onwards it's a new Glasgow and miles better. "

The leader of the Liberal Party might have been equally surprised if he had arrived at Glasgow's Central Station in the summer. Then he would have seen a continental touch with travellers enjoying the modern facilities of the new streamlined and efficient stations in Glasgow. But his surprise wouldn't stop there. In the words of Ian Jack in The Sunday Times magazine "Some marvellous and intriguing things have been happening to the city. Epidemics of stone-cleaning and tree-planting have transformed its former blackness into chequer-works of salmon pink, yellow and green. Old buildings have been burnished and refitted. Museums, delicatessens and wine-bars have opened, and thrive. New theatres occupy old churches. There are business centres, sports centres, heritage centres, arts centres. There are film-makers. There is even a nationally-acknowledged novelist or two. Its new appearance indeed persuades that it may become Britain's first major post industrial success." And little wonder.

Above: Woodside Terrace.
Top opposite: Blythswood Square.
Bottom left: Mews Arcade, West End.
Bottom right: Central Station.

A Royal Theatre

" I started my career as an actor in Glasgow just over 41 years ago. Since then I have been a regular visitor as a singer, actor and broadcaster. Glasgow folk are warm and friendly and very loyal to their entertainers. Now an important part of Glasgow's renaissance is an opera house of which any city could be proud. **"**

The only opera house in Scotland, the Theatre Royal is a jewel of a theatre. It is spectacular. It is a supreme example of Charles John Phipps' work, the acknowledged master of Victorian theatre design. A jewel in the crown of Glasgow which is almost certainly the best example of Victorian architecture in Europe. The theatre's Victorian rococo detail is delicate and restrained with its gracefully proportioned auditorium perhaps more in the late Georgian tradition. Reopened in 1975, its Victorian splendour is beautifully restored and most certainly plays an important part in Glasgow's renaissance.

Scottish Opera now enjoys an international reputation and between 1962 and 1982 no less than 1,800 performances of 75 different operas were given, four of which were specially commissioned. Sir Alexander Gibson who created Scottish Opera in 1962 has much to be proud of. During the 1983/84 season performances of The Magic Flute, The Golden Cockerel, Hansel and Gretel, L'Elisir d'Amore, La Boheme and L'Egisto were given, with My Fair Lady presented at Christmas using sets and costumes from London's West End.

Scottish Ballet who also has its home in Glasgow, is a regular performer at the Theatre Royal. It has been said that the growth of interest in Dance in Glasgow since the Theatre Royal reopened in 1975 is nothing short of phenomenal. And there are regular visits of Ballet Rambert, London Contemporary Dance Theatre and Sadlers Wells Royal Ballet to the Theatre. A proud record and proof that Glasgow can support seven to eight weeks of mainscale ballet, successfully.

Above: Scottish Ballet's The Nutcracker.
Left: The Theatre Royal.
Right: Scottish Opera's
The Marriage of Figaro.

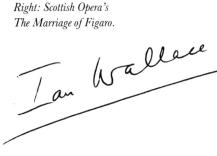

The road to Loch Lomond

Loch Lomond.
Almost certainly the most famous
inland waterway in the world.

" I do believe Glasgow's Miles Better nowadays. Years of grime have been enthusiastically washed away, and revealed honey-coloured sandstone architecture in all its amazing beauty.

The Burrell Gallery has leaped to the forefront of the public's imagination as a magnificent show-piece for the world's finest art, and of course Glasgow has more parks and recreation areas than any comparable European city. I know. I've played and walked in most of them! Other people will sing the praises of the new Exhibition Centre, but for me one of Glasgow's greatest attractions is the ease with which visitors and residents alike can reach the bonnie Campsie Fells to the north of the city, and the road to Loch Lomond, thence to the Highlands to the North West of the city. As for the glory of the nearby Firth of Clyde, that deserves a chapter all to itself! Finally, possibly the greatest riches which Glasgow possesses are its people. Warm and friendly, humorous, with the curiosity of the liveliest minds, they are quite unique. In the words of the song written for me many years ago by Gwen Lewis, my fellow-actress in Life with the Lyons, any visitor to Glasgow will find that:

'If you're rich, or if you're poor,
Or be ye up or doon,
You'll always find a welcome,
In dear old Glasgow Toon!'

Yes, there is no doubt about it, Glasgow really is Miles Better. " And there's no doubt few would disagree with Molly Weir on that.

Let Glasgow flourish by the preaching of the word

❝ It is the people who make Glasgow Miles Better. Warm, helpful and friendly, they make sure that no one remains a stranger in their great city, with its motto 'Let Glasgow flourish by the preaching of the word'. The civic pride and corporate confidence springs out of a deep sense of community. **❞**

A generous comment from The Very Reverend Dr Smith, fromer moderator of the General Assembly of the Church of Scotland on Glasgow's people. It's often reflected by visitors to the city. Glasgow people have always been Smiles Better, even in adversity, it's a great and friendly city!

Left: The Botanic Gardens.

On course in more ways than one

66 Glasgow's on course in more ways than one. **99**

The '85 British Open Champion knows more than most that Glasgow has made enormous strides forward in the last decade. His parents and family hail from Clober and Sandy's identification with Glasgow is therefore very much one of being at home when he is in Glasgow. Indeed, he gave up playing in one of the lucrative international tournaments recently, to make sure he played at Haggs Castle in The Glasgow Open. "And enjoyed every minute of it" he said.

In fact, there are actually no less than fourteen golf courses within the city boundaries, so it's really no wonder Glasgow people are keen on golf and are more than proud of their champion. In the words of the Scottish Daily Express when Sandy came to Glasgow shortly after winning The British Open Championship "Now Glasgow's Lyle's Better."

Scotland is of course the home of golf and the visitor to Glasgow can not only enjoy playing in one of Glasgow's fine golf courses but has to go no further than a short drive to be on the fairways of some of the finest golf courses in the world. Turnberry, Muirfield, Gleneagles, Troon, Prestwick to name a few!

On his visits to Glasgow Sandy will have seen the incredible transformation of a city now moving forward with a new confidence and vigour. The new motorway system for example can whisk him from one of Glasgow's new luxury hotels in the very centre of the city to the first tee at Haggs Castle in no less than five minutes! Hard to believe but true.

There are no less than fourteen golf courses within the city boundaries.

Sandy Lyle

A marvellous city. Unique and creative

❝ In a way, I feel like the song says that "I BELONG TO GLASGOW", because I treasure the love and ready friendship I receive from the Glaswegians, right from the very first time I played at the magnificent Glasgow Empire, rated second only to the London Palladium. It certainly was the 'Big Time' for me and before playing the Empire, I had heard so many stories about the Glasgow audiences, but being a Liverpudlian, I had at the back of my mind a feeling that it was a similar city. I was right — a city whose people, borne out of very hard times, who earned their bread and knew what a pound was, demanded and deserved one hundred percent performances — and I was ready for them.

My opening night was a very important one and had the most marvellous reception. The Glasgow audiences were ready for a one hundred percent performer and they seemed to like the kind of material which I 'socked' to them and they didn't hold back at all with their warm and generous applause.

The very next day, instead of sitting around waiting for the newspaper write ups, or just killing time, I went out and took myself around this great city to find out about it and to meet the people. During my walk, I took myself the entire length of Sauchiehall Street — because I had heard so much about it — and I was quite amazed because so many people stopped me on the street to say hello and to wish me luck and bid me welcome to their city.

It was, in fact, on that very day that I found, in a small sheet music shop, the song "Give Me The Moonlight Give Me The Girl" — I bought it for 1s 6d, used it that very night playing it with a top hat and cane. The audience lapped it up and this, of course, was the beginning of the image of Frankie Vaughan.

Since then, of course, I have had many similar very enjoyable times appearing at many of your lovely theatres and also, ten years ago, had the pleasure of being associated with the setting up of the Easterhouse project, which became a symbol of youth effort and a peace making move in an area that was torn apart by young gangs. Today there is a warm and good traditional feeling about the whole area.

As you see I have many reasons to be proud of my association with your marvellous city and its unique and creative atmosphere. **❞**

Above: Glasgow Empire Theatre in its hey-day.
Opposite: Sauchiehall Street as it is today.

Britain's Business Voice

" Glasgow's Miles Better because it is ideally located for Britain's Business Voice. **"**

Glasgow has one of the most efficient public transport systems in Britain. By road, rail, sea and air Glasgow is miles better. But it's miles better as Britain's business voice in more ways than one.

Why should Britain's industrialists stage their exhibitions and conferences in Glasgow? One good reason would be the Scottish Exhibition and Conference Centre, a brand new £36 million development. It's purpose built for the special needs of organisers, promoters, exhibitors and visitors and can match in quality and style anything in the rest of Europe. But perhaps the best reason of all is that Glasgow has so much to offer, as this book demonstrates conclusively. It's no coincidence that the CBI who after all is the corporate body that charts the course of Britain's industrial future recently held its annual conference in Glasgow and who commented on its great success. So much so that Glasgow has now been chosen again by the CBI for yet another annual conference. It's a compliment to all Glasgow's conference organisers.

Left: Recent CBI conference in Glasgow.
Above top: The new Scottish Exhibition
and Conference Centre in Glasgow.
Above: Seminar in progress in Glasgow for
The North Face, American manufacturers
of Alpine equipment.

Miles and miles of parks

Glasgow has no less than fifty-two parks and recreation areas in the city.

66 My early impression of Glasgow when I played there was that it was a rather dark and depressing place where open space seemed to be at a premium.

Recently while driving through I was staggered by the change. The parks in Glasgow are comparable to any other city. There seemed to be so many and all very well maintained. Yes, the parks are certainly what I think of as being Glasgow today. 99

In fact, Glasgow has more parks and recreation areas than any other similar-sized European city. In total there are fifty-two, one of which being Pollok Park which houses the world famous Burrell Collection. Miles Better!

Glasgow's now miles brighter

country. The University is now attractively floodlit in keeping with Glasgow's policy to light the city's important buildings. Now Glasgow is Miles Brighter. The Glasgow Institute of Architects say that the scheme to floodlight buildings of architectural interest, gives emphasis to the city's finest buildings and superb monuments.

Above: Strathclyde University.
Left: Glasgow University.

" My great grandfather was educated at the institute which has since become Strathclyde University and was there awarded a chemistry prize. I was also myself once Rector of Glasgow University. Glasgow will always have a warm place in my affections. **"**

If Lord Hailsham's great grandfather went to Strathclyde University today, one of Glasgow's two universities, he would find it a very different place. He would learn amongst other things that it is the biggest centre of marketing in Europe. Indeed, it is a little known fact that Scotland produces more university graduates per capita than any other European country. Glasgow's share in 1985 was 4,139. Glasgow University is one of the largest and oldest in Britain with the largest medical school and oldest engineering faculty in the

Hailsham.

Glasgow really does smile

Left: A friendly word from British Rail.
Centre: Enjoying one of Glasgow's
many swimming pools.
Right: The Ubiquitous Chip, Byres Road.
Below: The Suspension Bridge, Clyde Street.

66 Some cities shine, some cities shout, Glasgow really does smile. It isn't that it's got advantages and it isn't because it's self-satisfied — it's just that people in Glasgow would rather have a laugh than do anything. At least that is the way that the people of the City of Glasgow have always struck me — and a city is, after all, its people much more than its buildings or beauties. 99

Smiles better. Yes, there's no doubt the leader of Her Majesty's opposition is right. Even in difficult times Glasgow has never lost its friendly welcome and above all else our number one asset will always be our people. With Miles of Smiles.

Neil Kinnock

Tale of two cities

Ronnie Corbett

Left: Princes Street, Edinburgh.
Right: Glasgow University.

66 Dearly though I love Glasgow, my main allegiance has to be to Edinburgh — the place of my birth and education. **99**

Ronnie's thoughts are very laudable and who could argue with the sentiment. After all, Edinburgh is one of the world's most beautiful cities and every Scot is proud of Scotland's capital. Ronnie goes on to say "It would seem slightly disloyal to my native co-citizens of Edinburgh and the East Coast to be singing the praises of the West, maybe I should say Glasgow's miles Better because it's so near Edinburgh!" Which reminds one of another music hall comedian who once said "What I love about Edinburgh is the M8 motorway back to Glasgow."

Well, there's no doubt that there has been a centuries old friendly rivalry between the two great cities. And it's no bad thing. We Scots like to laugh at ourselves but will always rally our forces against "outsiders". In fact, the Glasgow's Miles Better campaign has been much admired in Edinburgh and everywhere else and is best summarised by the Scottish Daily Express when it said "The whole of Scotland has much to gain from this unique enterprise."

Communications. Miles better

Top left: The city's motorway system.
Bottom left: Concorde at Glasgow Airport.
Above top: Intercity streamlined service.
Above: A British Caledonian DC10.

66 Glasgow's Miles Better because of its excellent communications which link the city with the rest of the United Kingdom and the rest of the world. **99**

Where else can you get from airport to city centre in just 15 minutes? Very few places.

Glasgow's slogan is certainly more than relevant when it comes to communication, a vital and important link paramount to the prosperity of any major city with a dynamic outlook on life; and Glasgow certainly has that. It would probably be fair to say that Glasgow has a more impressive motorway system than most, linked as it is to the central system and routing directly through the centre of the city.

It would also be fair to say that Glasgow airport is Scotland's major airport with a through traffic of no less than 2.5 million passengers a year. Serviced by the major airlines whose activities like Glasgow are pushing ahead.

It's a miles better story with excellent inter-city rail connections and modern rail terminals and sea connections. And a modernised underground system in the city — where else will you find one of those? Miles better? We think so. And you will as well.

Scotland's cultural capital

Left: Christmas pantomime.
Opposite top: Kings Theatre.
Bottom left: Scottish Ballet.
Centre: The Citizens Theatre.
Right: Scottish Opera.

66 Glasgow is miles better because after the sad days when we lost the Metropole, the Empire, the new Metropole, the Alhambra, and thought we'd lost the Theatre Royal for good, we can now rejoice in six working theatres and in the knowledge that there are more theatre seats in Glasgow than any British city outside London itself. 99

Rejoicing indeed. Because Glasgow is a city with a cultural life and is rich in artistic heritage. The Kings Theatre, one of Stanley's favourites, was built in 1904 by Howard & Wyndham, beautifully refurbished in 1975 it has been host to musicals and international stars. It seats 1,800 and is particularly popular with Glaswegians at Christmas when the traditional pantomime is staged.

And surprisingly perhaps, the Theatre Royal is Scotland's only opera house. Not surprisingly, Glasgow is the home of Scottish Opera. Created by Sir Alexander Gibson in 1962, it became almost overnight Britain's most exciting post-war operatic venture. Now it has an enviable international reputation. Glasgow is also the home of Scottish Ballet, The Scottish Chamber Orchestra and Chorus, The Scottish National Orchestra and it has two repertory companies: the Scottish Theatre Company and the world famous Citizens Theatre Company, a pioneer in exciting new theatre and modern classics. Perhaps it's not surprising that Lady Marina Vaizey said in Highlife Magazine "The city is certainly Scotland's cultural capital." And then there is Mayfest, Glasgow's own festival every May. It's a showcase for Scottish writers, actors, performers and artists and after four short years of existence attracts theatre companies from all over the world. Glasgow's Miles Better.

Glasgow made itself Miles Better

66 Glasgow today is a cleaner, happier and more vigorous city. It's not just that the Miles Better campaign improved the image of the city — Glasgow responded to the challenge and actually made itself Miles Better. Once its name was synonymous with some of the unhappier aspects of life, particularly poverty; now it is coupled with commercial progress, enterprise and cultural initiative. **99**

It has been said that Glasgow could not have pursued its Glasgow's Miles Better campaign if the East End had remained as it was in the '70s. And it is in the East End where one of the most dramatic improvements has been made. The GEAR project on which over £200 million has been spent, has radically improved the physical environment, whilst there has been private house-building and rehabilitation of older property. Restoring listed buildings and landscaping has contributed to what is identified as a remarkable achievement.

The enterprise and commercial progress is a success story of partnership, of private and public sectors and where a great deal of credit must go to the Scottish Development Agency who have been inspirational and innovative. The SDA was set up by the Government with the objective of furthering economic development, to generate employment, to improve the environment and promote industrial efficiency. This it has done with considerable vigour and success and is today the envy of the United Kingdom.

Opposite: Clydesdale Bank, Buchanan Street.
Above top left: Clydeside Walkway.
Top centre: Templeton Business Centre.
Top right: New housing, Gallowgate.
Above left: Part of the GEAR project.
Above centre: A new office block.
Above right: Stone cleaning, West End.

World class art collection

Above: Rennie Mackintosh watercolour.
Right: Glasgow School of Art.
Far right: Christ of St. John
on the Cross.
Opposite centre: Rembrandt's Man in Armour.
Centre: Kelvingrove Art Gallery and Museum.

" Glasgow's Miles Better because of its quite outstanding world class art collection. "

Few people in the world can be unaware that Glasgow houses the Burrell Collection in its splendid new gallery in Pollok Park; but the treasures of Glasgow's many other galleries and museums are equally famous.

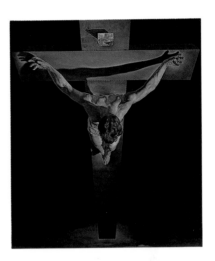

And there can be no more famous son of Glasgow than the renowned Charles Rennie Mackintosh.

Mackintosh was a man of quite remarkable achievement whose range was quite unique. His architecture has made him universally recognised as one of the great pioneers of modern architecture and design and much of his work can be seen in buildings in and around Glasgow. Outstanding examples being the Glasgow School of Art and the often quoted Cranston's Tearoom. When Mackintosh designed your house, he also designed the furniture, carpets, curtains and even the cutlery! He was also an artist of some considerable talent and is noted for his exquisite water colours and textile design. He also produced a brand of typographical style, not often referred to, that is unique to this day; it would be difficult to emulate such an original style.

The Hunterian Gallery housed at Glasgow University has as its principal feature a reconstruction on three floors of the main interiors from Rennie Mackintosh's home. The Gallery also has of importance, a collection of James McNeill Whistler's work and nineteenth and twentieth century Scottish paintings.

The Kelvingrove Art Gallery and Museum too has an astonishing collection of some of the world's finest masterpieces which includes Rembrandt's Man in Armour, Dali's Christ of St John of the Cross and Giorgione's The Adultress Brought before Christ. Kelvingrove Art Gallery is in itself a very beautiful building, and is considered to have one of the finest civic collections of art in Britain. Miles Better? Of course.

Then there's Pollok House, Haggs Castle, The Peoples Palace, The transport Museum. All of which demonstrating the considerable cultural treasures that are a big part of Glasgow's history.

New York, New York

Above: Great Western Road, Glasgow.
Above right: Manhattan, New York.
Right: Mr Pat Lally, leader Glasgow District Council in New York to promote the Glasgow's Miles Better campaign.
Opposite left: Manhattan, New York.
Opposite right: Pacific House, Glasgow.

66 Glasgow's new found energy reminds me of only one place, New York. 99

Anyone who has been to New York will know what Tom means. There's an indiscernible, underlying explosive excitement about the place; an energy that makes it like Glasgow. A get up and go quality. In fact, there are many similarities between New York and Glasgow. They obviously have a vitality in common; they are both leading art centres of the world; they both have highly successful promotional campaigns — I Love New York and our own Glasgow's Miles Better.

Glasgow believes in itself

66 Glasgow Smiles Better ... because it believed that it was miles better. **99**

Former Secretary of State for the Environment Michael Heseltine's thoughts are well founded. With the close involvement and understanding of the problems of the inner cities, he knows that confidence plays a major role in achievement; and that the first principle in any enterprise is to believe in yourself. The first achievement of the Miles Better campaign was to rally the forces and revive the inherent pride that every Glaswegian has in his city. Success breeds success and Glasgow is now building on it.

Miles of sporting people

*Glasgow on the move
in more ways than one!*

❝ Glasgow's Miles Better because it welcomes sporting people from around the world. **❞**

Glasgow certainly is into sport in a big way, particularly it would seem at weekends when runners of all ages can be seen in the parks and in the streets! No doubt many of whom are out practising for the Glasgow Marathon. The Marathon is now the third largest in the world coming second only to New York and London. It's an achievement that is helping to put Glasgow miles ahead. But then Glasgow has always had a keen interest in sport and today the city boasts five magnificent sports centres, ten athletic tracks and no less than sixty-one excellent swimming pools.

Dear Green Place

Left: Botanic Gardens.
Opposite left: Pollok Park.
Opposite top: Victoria Park.
Centre: Kelvin Walkway.

" The transformation is complete. 'No mean city' is 'The Dear Green Place' again. Congratulations Glasgow. **"**

There are few visitors to Glasgow today who would be likely to identify Glasgow as 'No mean city' and indeed some would wonder how a city renowned for its generosity and friendliness could ever have been labelled in this way. Stanley Baxter quipped 'Never a mean city' would have been more appropriate!

In fact, the very name of the city has its origins in the Celtic words "Dear Green Place". And today few cities in the world can match Glasgow for the sheer beauty of its parks and open spaces, nor can they match the astonishing quantity of Glasgow's parks and recreation grounds. It's no wonder some have called Glasgow the Garden City of Europe, a phrase which will come into its own in 1988 when the Garden Festival is hosted by Glasgow. It will be the UK's biggest single consumer event of 1988, an important international occasion when more than four million visitors will be welcomed. It will be a unique opportunity to see that Glasgow IS Miles Better.

This book explained. A "Dear John" letter

Robbie's letter has prompted an explanation of what this book is about and indeed how it came about. The idea was born from a desire to do something to help the famine relief in Ethiopia and perhaps, at the same time produce an all-embracing book on Glasgow which for some reason never seems to have been done.

It will also demonstrate Glasgow's willingness not only to help itself but to help others. And it will show the world that Glasgow's Miles Better.

The author having conceived the idea wrote to the celebrities in all walks of life who have contributed to this book, and asked them quite simply to give a quote on why they thought Glasgow's Miles Better. The response, as this book proves, was phenomenal. Robbie had numerous thoughts on Glasgow with a number of suggestions for his quote but the whole spirit of his letter seemed to be worth sharing, and it has therefore been reproduced in full . . .

66 Dear John

What's it like getting a "Dear John" every day of the year? A mite depressing I shouldn't wonder! First, let me apologise for the delay in replying to your highly flattering letter, you silver-tongued bastard you. The reasons are legion. I've moved house, I've been very ill, and I'm a lazy slob.

It's hard to know where to begin when describing why "Glasgow's Miles Better". I could tell you with genuine tears in my eyes that I remember seeing weans with no shoes in the Gorbals, and of walking in front of my old man's car with a torch in

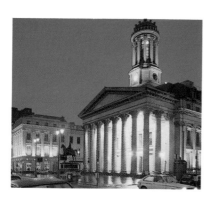

my hand trying to follow the tram lines home during those terrible smogs. The total terror of hearing "Cumbie ya bass" and the noise of breaking glass at the dancing during the sixties. The terrible roaring drunkenness that used to result from repressive drinking hours: in short, whine on for hours why Glasgow IS Miles Better: I

also believe, like most post-industrial centres it would be miles better off without a Tory government whose eyes go out of focus beyond the Edgeware Road: however, don't get me started on that one!

If you are using strong visuals on this one, I would say that the massive clean-up of the tenements is a winner, so what about "John Betjeman's view that Glasgow has some of the finest architecture in Europe, is now abundantly, clearly, true, now that we can see it in all its detail" accompanied by a pic of The Exchange?

Or alternatively: "The Glasgow School of Art, Mackintosh's masterpiece, a symbol of Glasgow's historic ability to embrace the new." A bit Readers Digest perhaps, but you can bet your last luncheon voucher it would never have been built in Edinburgh, Manchester, Liverpool or London.

Third and last: "It's impressive and rare to find a city that has obviously spent so much time and thought for the pedestrian in the inner city." I think that's quite relevant, because for example, it's almost impossible to walk about in

London, where the car is king. You could have a pic of the pedestrian walkways in Buchanan Street or the Street of Willows even. I shall be up in the Dear Green Place from March 17 to September 27 this year filming, so if you want me to help in any capacity at all, just leave a message at Andy Park's office at BBC, Queen Margaret Drive, and I'll let you buy me a small, dry sherry. Good luck, I think it's a great idea. **"**

Sincerely,

Left: Buchanan Street.
Bottom left: The Stirling Library.
Centre: Glasgow School of Art.
Right: The Mitchell Library.

I extend warm congratulations to Scotland's industrial capital on the outstanding success of the "Glasgow's Miles Better" campaign, which is doing so much to project the true image of the city throughout the country and indeed the world. I am particularly pleased that it has not been seen as a short term effort, but that it will continue as a long term project. Much hard work has gone into this very worthwhile endeavour, and I thank all who have played a part in it.

It is impossible not to be impressed by Glasgow. It is a city which is proud, and rightly so, of its history, its splendid architecture so lovingly restored and cleaned, its world renowned reputation for the arts, its academic excellence, and the traditional skills of its people. But it is also a city which does not fear change; and is prepared to look to the future. That is why it has been swift to seize the opportunity to innovate, to take up the challenge of the new technology and to look to the methods and products of the new age. In doing so it has ensured that it will continue to flourish in the years to come as successfully as it has done in the years gone by.

Glasgow is very alive

66 Glasgow is very alive and that's how it makes you feel. **99**

Sir Peter Hall is a man who is constantly on the move around the world's capitals on National Theatre business. His perceptions, finely tuned by virtue of his profession are perhaps more valid than most and his feeling that Glasgow is alive is in many ways confirmation of a vitality that is forcing Glasgow forward. It is an extension of the city's bustling philosophy that Glasgow certainly is Miles Better.

Peter Hall

Friendly, fun and anything but dour

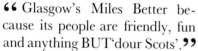

❝ Glasgow's Miles Better because its people are friendly, fun and anything BUT 'dour Scots'. **❞**

There's a strange idea lurking somewhere within the Sassenach mind that Scots are dour. So it's nice to know that Jean Rook who knows a thing or two about fun people, thinks that Glasgow folk are friendly and fun. A high compliment from Jean for which we are very pleased and a little bit proud. We will always give her a very warm welcome when she's in Glasgow.

It's easy to gloss over the cracks in this world and of course we know Glasgow is not perfect but we also know that every single person who lives and works in Glasgow is striving to project our new image that Glasgow's Miles Better. And indeed it is, in almost every respect. It's good to know that Mr Happy is up front reflecting Glasgow's big, big smile.

Jean Rook

*Miles and miles of smiles
that's Glasgow's welcome
to the world.*

Like Londoners we know our football

Below: Celtic, Queen's Park.
Below right: Partick Thistle, Dumbarton.
Bottom left: Clyde, Motherwell.
Bottom right: Rangers, Celtic.
Opposite page: Scotland, England.

" To me Glasgow's Miles Better because of the friendliness I have always encountered in a much maligned city. I have always found Glaswegians full of humour and of course cheek – exactly like the London Eastenders. Like us too, they certainly know their football. "

How dare Jimmy Greaves say we're cheeky. From a guy who scored all those cheeky goals against Scotland! But of course he's right and some of his cheeky goals were really great; and greatly admired too. Of course, Jimmy has played often in the national football stadium at Hampden Park which is only minutes from the centre of Glasgow. It's the home of the Queen's Park Club, the only amateur club which plays in a senior league in Scotland and has a permanent place in the history of Scottish football. In fact, the Scottish Football Association was formed in 1873 at a meeting in Dewar's Hotel in Glasgow, called by Queen's Park for the purpose of arranging a Scottish Cup competition.

There are no less than five senior Clubs in Glasgow – Clyde, Partick Thistle, Queen's Park and the two most famous clubs in Scotland, Rangers and Celtic.

Some would say the two most famous clubs in the world! One thing is certain however and that is the Rangers stadium at Ibrox is probably by far the finest in Europe and must rank as one of the world's best. Miles Better? There's not much doubt Jimmy.

Jimmy Greaves

The largest public library in Europe

" Glasgow's Miles Better because of the superb architecture it has inherited. **"**

Glasgow's inheritance of splendid Victorian architecture has now taken on a bright new look as the great buildings all round the city are lovingly and carefully cleaned and restored to their former glory. The city has become a place of architectural pilgrimage to tourists around the world. The Mitchell Library in North Street is a superb example of Glasgow's new brightness. Indeed as a Scottish Nationalist member of parliament Donald Stewart will probably know that it is not only the largest public reference library in Europe but it also has the largest collection of books on Robert Burns in the world. Glasgow's Miles Better!!!

*The Mitchell Library
in North Street beautifully
floodlit, showing its
magnificent architecture.*

Combining the new with the old

Below: Kent Road, near Charing Cross.
Opposite top left: Scottish Television, Cowcaddens.
Bottom left: Pacific House, Wellington Street.
Bottom centre: Central Station.
Right: Waterloo Street.

66 Glasgow's Miles Better because it has combined so successfully the new with the old. Scottish Television's studio centre not only occupies a prime city centre site but it keeps alive the name and tradition of one of old Glasgow's most famous streets – Cowcaddens. **99**

Scottish Television's headquarters are of course based in Glasgow, as readers of this book will have come to expect. It will seem that every major commercial enterprise as well as the endless list of cultural and artistic centres have their homes in Glasgow; and that is not too far from the truth.

Glasgow is very rich in assets in almost every direction. But to take Sir Campbell Fraser's point that Glasgow's Miles Better because it has successfully combined the new with the old is a factor of which the city's planners can be justifiably proud.

Whilst it is now a delight to see Glasgow's beautiful Victorian buildings restored and gleaming in their splendour, one can see right alongside them brand new office buildings which blend with the environment. Tasteful and gentle persuasion have produced an attractive blend of the new which is acceptable in retaining a traditional heritage; important aspects of a quality of life that is paramount to every Glaswegian who treasures the heritage handed down through centuries.

Glasgow is, after all, one of the best examples of Victorian architecture in the world and is there for all the world to enjoy and share with the people of Glasgow.

It's no wonder we have a lot to smile about as Glasgow emerges into a new era. It's an exciting era full of promise for everyone's future.

Gordon Jackson

66 When I revisit Glasgow now, of course I'm always very impressed – so many changes since I was a boy there – and all for the better! But what hasn't changed is the warmth and friend- liness of the Glasgow people! They're so kind and considerate and cheeky. Yes, Glasgow's miles better, because Glasgow SMILES better! 99

Gordon's comments are of course the comments that Glas- gow people have come to know and take great pride in. We are without doubt a friendly city and we particularly welcome strangers. We have always been happy to share our riches with our fellow man, even when we didn't have too many. It's a quality that every Glaswegian is proud of. Cheeky? Yes we are that too. It's something that has plenty of goodwill behind it and indeed

emphasises our ability to laugh at ourselves. This is perhaps one good reason why Mr Happy has been virtually adopted by the city. Because he's a lot of fun and pretty cheeky as he jaunts along at the head of the Glasgow's Miles Better campaign.

It's no wonder that over a million car stickers happily adorn the rear windows of Glaswegians' cars. When Glasgow's on the move, it puts everything behind it!

The Glasgow's Miles Better campaign in action. Lord Provost Robert Gray in the driving seat.

The Gorbals makes a marvellous surprise

Janet Brown [signature]

Now there is a transformation that has put the smile back on Glasgow's face.

❝ On my last visit to Glasgow, I took a trip round the Gorbals and I really got the most marvellous surprise. The Gorbals makes a marvellous surprise. **❞**

Janet Brown is one of Britain's top impersonators but she would certainly realise that anyone making a trip today to the Gorbals in the East End of Glasgow, would not be seeing an impersonation. Because the changes there demonstrate a transformation that has put a smile back on Glasgow's face. The Glasgow Eastern Renewal Project (GEAR) has seen to that. There is a recognition that the project is probably the most comprehensive and advanced urban renaissance scheme in Western Europe. The depressing image, furthered by Film and Television companies, that here was a perfect location for scenes of urban deprevation, is no longer. That image is as outdated as the steam engine. So we hope the film companies will come back in their masses to project to the world the remarkable change for the better, the real reality of Glasgow. In the words of Andrew Collier in the Daily Telegraph "The reality is that Glasgow is a beautiful city, full of culture, worthy architecture and some of the friendliest people in Europe."

Now there is an environment that people want to live and work in. More than 1,000 owner occupier houses have been built in the East End recently, the first private homes to be built there for 50 years; and a further 2,000 are planned. There are trees and flowers, planting and landscaping. Next time Janet comes back she'll be even more surprised because Glasgow is still moving ahead with numerous improvements, almost everywhere you turn. Now we have a city of marvellous surprises.

One of Britain's best shopping centres

Below: Argyle Arcade.
Right top: The Briggate.
Centre: The Victorian Antique Village.
Bottom: Design Centre, St. Vincent Street.
Main picture: Frasers, Buchanan Street.

" Each year during our Autumn break in Scotland, my wife Kathy insists on a visit to Glasgow. This is a great worry to me as I know she finds it one of the best shopping centres in Britain. Not only for the goodies she always finds but for the friendliness and helpfulness of the shop assistants. And I think our bank manager worries too. **"**

Glasgow has always been known as a very good shopping centre. But Glasgow has more than just superb shops, it has led the way with pedestrian shopping precincts, where you can walk down its world famous Sauchiehall Street, Buchanan Street and Argyle Street and not encounter a single car; but you may encounter an interesting piece of sculpture or beautifully planted trees and shrubs in strategically placed tubs! A new environment.

Architecture without parallel

66 Glasgow's Miles Better because, in spite of some regrettable losses, it is the finest Victorian city in the world. The ensemble of domestic, university and church architecture of this period is without parallel. **99**

Roy Jenkins as the Member of Parliament for Glasgow's Hillhead has first hand knowledge of the city's heritage. To visit the city is a pleasurable experience; to live and work in the city as Roy Jenkins does is a bonus. A man of his distinction is of course a bonus for Glasgow as he more than most will appreciate the surroundings.

The influence of "Greek" Thomson and Charles Rennie Mackintosh are very much in evidence in Glasgow, one of the few cities in Britain which can lay a claim to a strong local tradition in architecture. A special bonus.

Right: Glasgow University.
Bottom right: Haggs Castle.
Below: Pollok House.
Opposite top left: Glasgow School of Art.
Opposite bottom: City Chambers.
Opposite right: Ramshorn Church.

Friendly people

*Kenny Dalglish
is never happier than
when he is giving
encouragement.*

66 Glasgow is special to me because it is my home town and the people are very friendly. **99**

Kenny's words are probably the truest reflection of any Glaswegian's thoughts on his home town. Now a freeman of the City of Glasgow, Kenny has had an illustrious career and Glaswegians around the world are proud of his achievements.

And although Kenny has spent much of his playing career away from home, he is one of the most popular soccer stars ever to wear a Scottish jersey. A true gentleman on and off the field and an inspiration to youngsters everywhere. No one anywhere could do more for the up and coming stars of tomorrow. If there's anything that Kenny can do for a schoolboy or youth team, he's never happier than when he's giving encouragement.

Energy, vitality, imagination, commitment

66 The energy and vitality of Glasgow shows precisely how cities can renew themselves by effort, imagination and commitment even in times of dire economic distress. Moreover, it is a city which has transcended the sectarian divisions which bedeviled its past. **99**

The Archbishop of Canterbury's words are flattering to every person in Glasgow. They reflect the qualities that will move Glasgow rapidly to the position of a city that will again be admired and emulated the world over.

Glasgow's people are the ambassadors for a very great city and are no longer prisoners of its past. They now display a pride and confidence. Look at the smiles in our picture of Pollok's new leisure pool, the only one of its kind in Scotland. Glasgow's self-image has now taken a giant step forward.

Anything is possible

Left: The Buttery Restaurant.
Opposite top: The Grosvenor Hotel.
Opposite centre: The Albany Hotel.
Bottom left: The Holiday Inn.
Bottom right: The Hospitality Inn.

❞ The first time I was in Glasgow it was particularly evident that the Luftwaffe had been the night before. The city was devastated — the population deeply depressed. I thought of coming out in sympathy by vandalising my hotel room. That was in 1972. Now you have proved it is possible to seize urban blight by the lapels and heave it against the nearest wall. How good to see that this traditional Glaswegian greeting has worked. You have in the American idiom, turned Glasgow round. You have proved that anything is possible. I wish you could do the same for me. ❟

The next time Willie's in Glasgow his room may be in one of the city's brand new hotels. And he could step out in the evening and take a stroll along one of our new walk-ways or visit an exquisite new restaurant.

A great place to live and work

“ The rebuilding of Glasgow's East End has brought about the renaissance of one of Europe's great cities. I much admire the energy and imagination that has gone into its rebuilding, and has a very encouraging future. ”

Glasgow's Miles Better, it's a great place to live and work is a line that appears as a slogan on hundreds of thousands of Glaswegians' cars, proving fairly conclusively that their inherent pride in their city is strong and vibrant. This is reflected in Shirley Williams' book "A job to live" when she says "The old stone tenements have been gutted and rebuilt inside; derelict sites have been turned into parks and gardens, or used for low-rise pleasantly designed houses and bungalows; an old factory building, the Templeton carpet factory, has been converted into a

business centre containing workshops and offices. Throughout the East End the best has been saved and re-used, the worst pulled down and replaced with human-scale buildings. People now want to live and work there."

There is very little doubt that the GEAR (Glasgow Eastern Area Renewal) project is one of very considerable success and there is no doubt that a very great deal of credit must go to the Scottish Development Agency for the transformation. Their objectives were to concentrate on improving and rehabilitating the local environment with emphasis on the new industrial areas of electronics, health care, energy-related technology and advanced engineering.

GEAR is a triumph of a co-ordinated action where relative flexibility has encouraged local commitment and where private house-building has been encouraged. Landscaping, cleaning buildings, and renovating listed buildings have all contributed to that success. Indeed the partnership of private and public sectors has been a contributory factor in the success of the Glasgow's Miles Better project.

The exciting GEAR initiative has produced dramatic improvements in the environment and was backed by an expenditure of over £200 million. It is a shining example of what can be done if the will is there to do it. But whilst the East End project is successful its motivating principles are to be seen all round the city. Anyone who walked the length of Maryhill Road ten years ago would be astonished at the incredible transformation that is Maryhill Road today. Delightful new houses line the road, landscaping much in evidence, with trees, greenery, flowers and shrubs. Maryhill Road like the East End of Glasgow is certainly miles better. But it doesn't stop there.

"It's not surprising to read in the Daily Telegraph recently that "Glasgow is a beautiful city, full of culture, worthy architecture and some of the friendliest people in Europe – even the English are starting to realise this.Recognition of the fact that Glasgow's depressing image is outdated and totally incorrect is due largely to the huge image-building campaign combining efforts from the public and private sectors." ... Miles Better? Yes.

Housing co-operatives

*Above: His Royal Highness The Prince of Wales
on a recent visit to Glasgow.
Left: London Road improvements.
Centre: New Housing in the East End.*

The following is an extract from His Royal Highness The Prince of Wales' speech to ScotBIC in November 1985, a welcome and very helpful appraisal of the facts.

"In Glasgow, the Easterhouse and Govanhill housing developments have done a great deal with housing co-operatives and housing associations to try and re-generate and renovate the run-down housing there. But one of the things I have discovered is that if you can improve peoples' conditions in which they live, and enable them themselves to take a hand in deciding what kind of surroundings they want to live in and what kind of houses they want, with porches, windows and everything else, and gardens, but just the fact that they have been able to take a hand in this and have been shown, as I have said before, how to find their way through the red tape and the legislation and so on, then it is quite extraordinary how they discover talents they didn't know they had. And that can I think very often spill over, and I have seen it happen, into enterprise and people setting up their own enterprises where before they would never have believed it possible to do so."

The most interesting city in the British Isles

Left: The Burrell building.
Right: The Glasgow marathon.
Opposite left: The motorway system.
Opposite right: Scottish Exhibition
and Conference Centre.

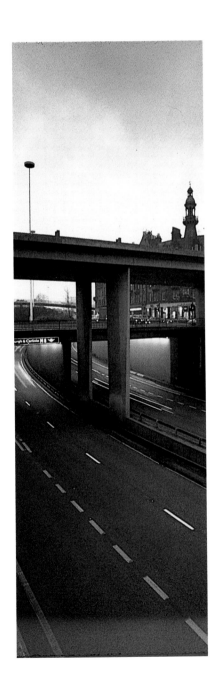

" Thank God Glasgow is at last beginning to throw off the last century and getting itself in shape for the next. **"**

As Editor of The Sunday Times Andrew Neil is a man with his finger on the pulse and is of considerable importance in the business of communicating the facts on Glasgow to an influential audience. The following quote recently appeared in the Sunday Times Colour Magazine "Glasgow has achieved a tremendous turnaround in the last five years. The catchy Glasgow's Miles Better ad campaign has helped remove the grimy, crime-ridden image: more people are realising that Glasgow is perhaps the most interesting city in the British Isles." And soon more will know.

Andrew F Neil

Peace on Earth

"Peace on Earth". This was the sentiment expressed on the cover of the Lord Provost's Christmas card in 1982. The card was designed by Struthers and was the forerunner to the Miles Better campaign.

It showed the Pope shaking hands with the Moderator of the General Assembly of the Church of Scotland. And after his historic visit to Scotland The Pope is on record as saying "The warmest reception I have received outside of Poland, was in Scotland." There certainly was miles of smiles in Glasgow when he visited Bellahouston Park. Archbishop Winning on his visit to The Pope on St Andrew's Day in 1982 reported that he was greeted by The Pope with his hand placed on his heart, saying "Bellahouston, I still have all that here." A cherished memory.

The Royal Scottish Academy of Music

George Maunger

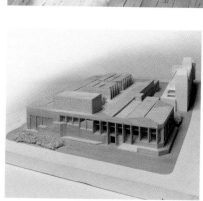

Below: Conductor Neeme Järvi.
Bottom left: The new building
(early scale model).
Opposite left: Scottish National Orchestra.
Opposite centre: Promenade concert.
Opposite right: The new building.

❝ Glasgow's Miles Better because of its remarkable new building for the Royal Scottish Academy of Music which is being built by the Scottish Education Department for one of Britain's leading music colleges. ❞

Former Secretary of State for Scotland George Younger has a long association with Glasgow and in his years at the Scottish Office has seen many remarkable changes for the better in Glasgow. He has seen the city's development in close association with the SDA's numerous projects taking shape; he has seen the Burrell Collection being rehoused and its magnificent Gallery opened by Her Majesty The Queen; he has seen the Scottish Exhibition and Conference Centre opened in Glasgow; he has seen a new vibrant emergence of the Glaswegians' inherent pride.

Those who belong believe

Diana Rigg

Opposite top left: A Glasgow smile.
Opposite top right: The Holiday Inn.
Opposite bottom left: Fishmonger.
Opposite bottom right: Glasgow Highland Games.
Top: Third Eye Centre.
Left: Her Majesty the Queen
in George Square.
Above: Funfair in the park.

❝ Why is Glasgow Miles Better? Because those who belong to Glasgow believe in Glasgow. **❞**

It would certainly be very difficult to convince anyone outside of Glasgow if the people themselves did not believe it. They live and work in Glasgow and can see for themselves that Glasgow's Miles Better than it was. And they can smile along with Mr Happy because they know too that Glasgow Smiles Better. They have shown this by the almost unprecedented display of pride in their city, by placing over a million car stickers on their cars that proclaim the message loud and clear that their city is Miles Better. Perhaps a little bit tongue in cheek with maybe just a hint of suspicion that what they are saying to the world is that now Glasgow's Miles Better than anywhere else. Is there any doubt?

A refreshing freedom

Right: The Motorway System.
Top left: Ladywell, East End.
Centre: Strathclyde University Campus.
Bottom: Townhead community development.

66 Glasgow's urban renewal, using public and private enterprise, has a refreshing freedom of dogma about it. Other cities could copy it with considerable benefit, **99** says Dr David Owen.

The partnership of private and public sectors has undoubtedly been one of the keys to opening the route to a successful formula which is now paying handsome dividends. Glasgow is doing something for itself and is certainly being noticed. The Economist said "Glasgow has plenty to shout about, but its greatest asset is its noisy new self-confidence. With help from its friends, public sector and private, and a past that actually left a lot beside dirt and dud industry, Glasgow is showing that if you believe enough in yourself others in time will come to believe the same proving that you are right."

This glorious British City

Russell Grant

Left: An appreciative audience.
Below: At the Citizens Theatre.
Bottom: Scottish Opera.
Opposite top: Kings Theatre.
Opposite bottom: Evening Times,
Albion Street.

66 Having spent many years working in Glasgow, I remember the warmth and friendliness of the people and my happy days at the Kings Theatre and Scottish Opera House with great pleasure.

I am certainly very pleased to be able to continue my links with this glorious British city through my work for the Evening Times. 99

Of all the media who have contributed enormously to the success of the Glasgow's Miles Better campaign probably the Evening Times have been the campaign's greatest champion. Indeed, they are on record as saying "The Miles Better campaign has been one of the biggest marketing successes of the last decade. A thoroughly professional programme has had the enthusiastic support of all sections of the community." A big success story.

Glasgow gives hope to other areas in Britain

Above: West of Scotland Science Park.
Opposite top left: Strathclyde University.
Bottom left: Glasgow University.
Opposite right: Glasgow College of Building & Printing.

66 There is a strong link between ICI and Glasgow in that at the beginning of the century, one of our founding companies, Nobel Industries, had its offices there. Many of today's customers, the Universities and colleges and the city's commercial centre, ensure that link lives on. The city's regeneration gives hope to other areas in Britain and wider afield, for it shows the need for both traditional and modern businesses to survive and develop, if our great cities are to live. Let Glasgow flourish! 99

Sir John Harvey-Jones is chairman of ICI, one of Britain's biggest businesses and his reference to Glasgow giving hope to other areas of Britain is becoming more evident every day as other cities like Bradford and Liverpool send delegations to Glasgow to investigate the campaign success.

The Garden Festival. A look into the future

66 Glasgow's Miles Better because it looks into the future and makes it happen. 99

Being one of the world's golfing superstars Tony Jacklin can testify to the fact that if you want something to happen in this world, then you have to make it happen. And things are happening in Glasgow! There will be no greater event than in 1988 when Glasgow hosts the Garden Festival, the biggest single consumer event of 1988 when an estimated four million visitors will visit this unique shop window for Glasgow. The Festival will be an achievement for Glasgow, and indeed its existence is already an achievement for the Miles Better campaign with the Daily Telegraph reporting that it has helped to persuade the Government to let the City of Glasgow stage the National Garden Festival in 1988.

*Festival Theme Parks
from left to right:
Recreation and Sport.
Science and Technology.
Health and Wellbeing.
Water and Maritime.
Plants and Food.
Land and Scenery.*

Announcing the Garden Festival.
From left:
Selina Scott.
Billy Connolly.
Mr Alan Stewart MP.
Lord Provost Robert Gray.
Sir Norman Macfarlane.
Mr Alan Devereux.
Mr Robin Duthie.

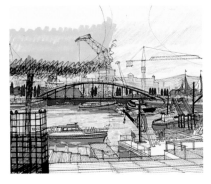

Bonnie and Clyde

Above: Sunset on the Clyde.
Top left: Kelvin walkway.
Centre left: The QE2, New York.
Opposite left: The Waverley.
Opposite right: Clyde walkway.

“ Glasgow's Miles Better because salmon are now running up the Clyde again. **”**

Times have changed. The Clyde is pure again and the fish are back. The Krankies whose business is putting smiles on people's faces know that Glasgow can smile with a quiet confidence that the river that launched a thousand ships is clean, and is right at the centre of Glasgow's renaissance.

The river that launched QE2, the world's finest ship, which thousands of Glaswegians helped to build, has been transformed. Now you can take a stroll along the Clyde walkways, you can see attractive riverside housing, you can enjoy the landscaping, you can see the new Scottish Exhibition and Conference Centre, the most modern of its kind in Europe. A great multi-purpose complex, it has covered exhibition halls, conference facilities and a 10,000 seat arena. It has shops, restaurants and will soon have a bridge over the river linking it to the Garden Festival site which in 1988 will provide Scotland with the event of the century. And who knows, from one of the floating restaurants you might even see a salmon leaping.

Glasgow looks better, feels better, sounds better

66 Glasgow's Miles Better . . . well it might be for you but not for me. You see I don't live here any more and so every time I come back, although it looks better, feels better, and sounds better than it used to, I just get plain jealous cos I'm not here to enjoy it. So you see, it might be miles better for you but for me it's actually miles worse. 99

B A Robertson's words probably express the feelings of all Glaswegians when they return to their native city from foreign parts. They can see the city has been transformed in just about every way. They can see the landscaping, the tree-planting, the walkways taking shape, new housing pleasantly overlooking the river, new hotels, new restaurants, shopping precincts. They can feel the city pulsating with excitement; they can feel the vigour. There isn't much doubt, it's all there. Miles Better! You could perhaps say that Glasgow is very much on song.

Opposite: Central Station.
Top left: Garnethill.
Top right: Kelvin Walkway.
Bottom left: The Scottish Exhibition and Conference Centre.
Bottom right: The Copthorne Hotel, George Square.

The finest debating society in Britain

❝ Glasgow's Miles Better because its ancient university has the finest Debating Society in Great Britain, which continues to produce outstanding public servants for the whole nation. **❞**

It would take a lot more pages than one of Jeffrey Archer's blockbusters to name the many, many famous national and international figures who have studied at Glasgow University. Leaders in all walks of life and all fields of activity. People like A J Cronin, John Logie Baird, Lord Kelvin, Sir William McKeown, Ramsay MacDonald, Alistair MacLean, James Watt and Adam Smith. It's an impressive and endless list. It has often been said that one of Scotland's largest exports is brainpower, and few are in any doubt of the enormous contribution Glasgow has made to the world in that direction. It's a proud tradition from a city with a world outlook and ambassadors in every corner of the globe, proclaiming the message that Glasgow really is Miles Better.

Glasgow now has a wealth of riches and is growing in economic strength every day. It's a Glasgow that Adam Smith who wrote "The Wealth of Nations" would have taken great pride in.

Jeffrey Archer

Above: Glasgow University Library.
Left: Adam Smith's statue in the Hunterian Museum.
Opposite top left: The Adam Smith Building.
Top centre: The Boyd Orr Building.
Top right: The Hetherington Building.
Bottom left: University graduates.
Bottom right: The East Quadrangle.

HMS Glasgow's Miles Better

Michael Havers

HMS Glasgow.
The only ship in the Royal Navy
with its own corporate identity.

❝ Ever since I visited as a sailor in the war, I have always thought Glasgow was the friendliest city to strangers in the world. ❞

Sir Michael Havers is reflecting the views of people the world over. It is quite remarkable how often Glasgow's people are identified as friendly to strangers; it's probably one of our greatest assets. Glasgow does really smile better seems to be echoed round the world. In fact, it is more than echoed, as Sir Michael as a former navy man will be interested to know. Because the campaign's message is carried by the Royal Navy's HMS Glasgow wherever she goes. In the words of her captain "We are proud to carry Glasgow's message, it is a terrific boost for morale."

Everyone who witnesses HMS Glasgow arriving in port will see the unusual spectacle of Her Majesty's guided missile destroyer lowering her gangplank with the message painted in 4 ft high letters that proclaims our slogan "HMS Glasgow's Miles Better." So the whole world will be left in no doubt as far as the Royal Navy is concerned that things have been happening in Glasgow. Thank you Royal Navy, now HMS Glasgow's Miles Better.

The last word

66 Marvellous. **99**

    It's a sentiment expressed by Lord Provost Robert Gray when he refers to Glasgow as a great place for anyone to live and work.